THIS BOOK BELONGS TO

Small Preview Of What's Inside

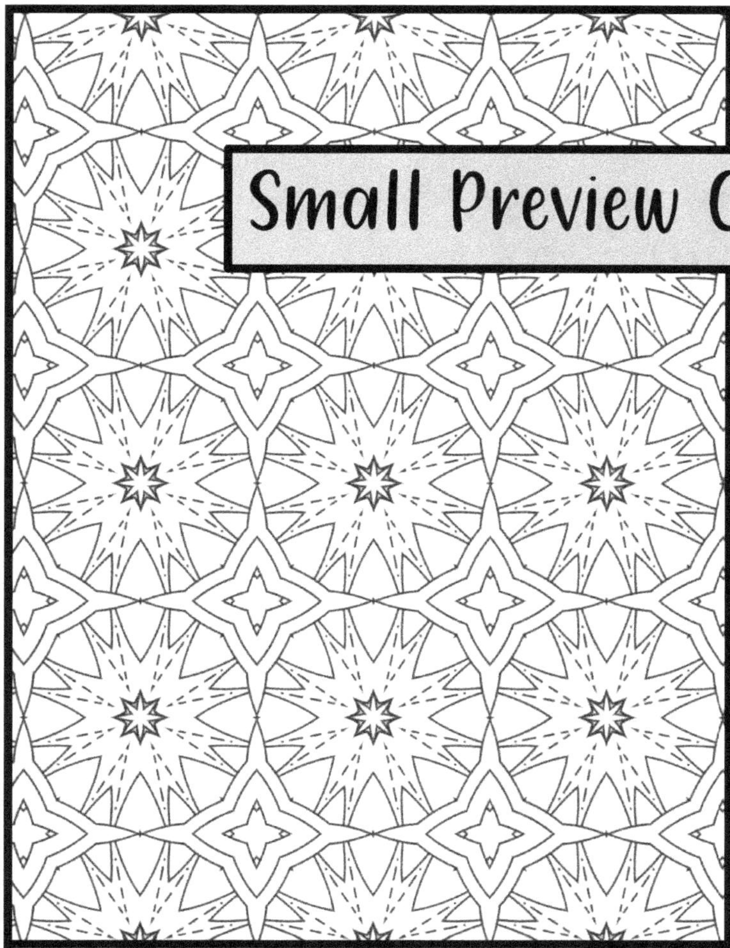

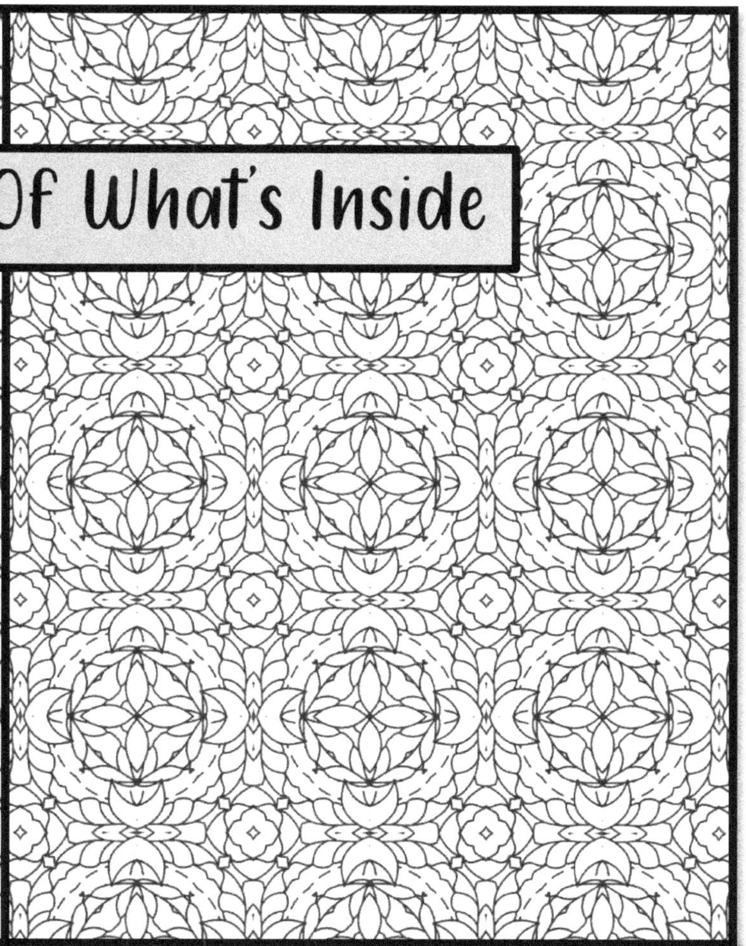

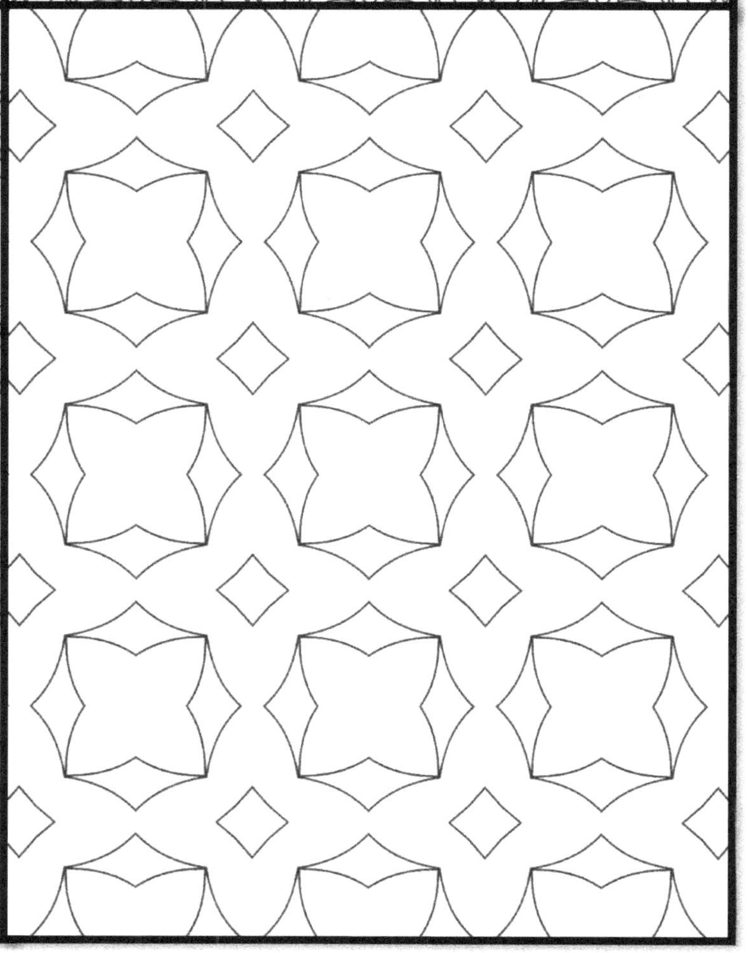

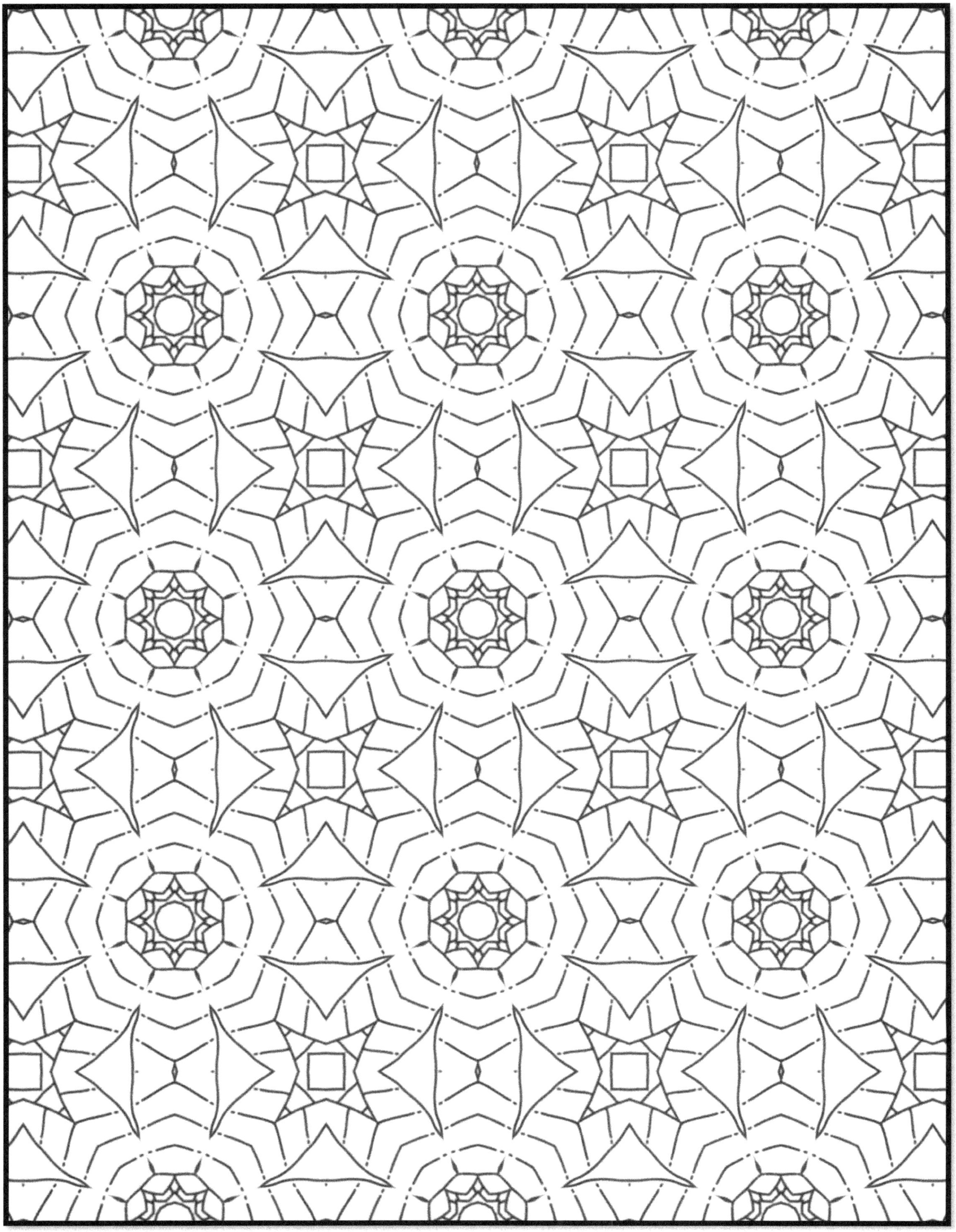

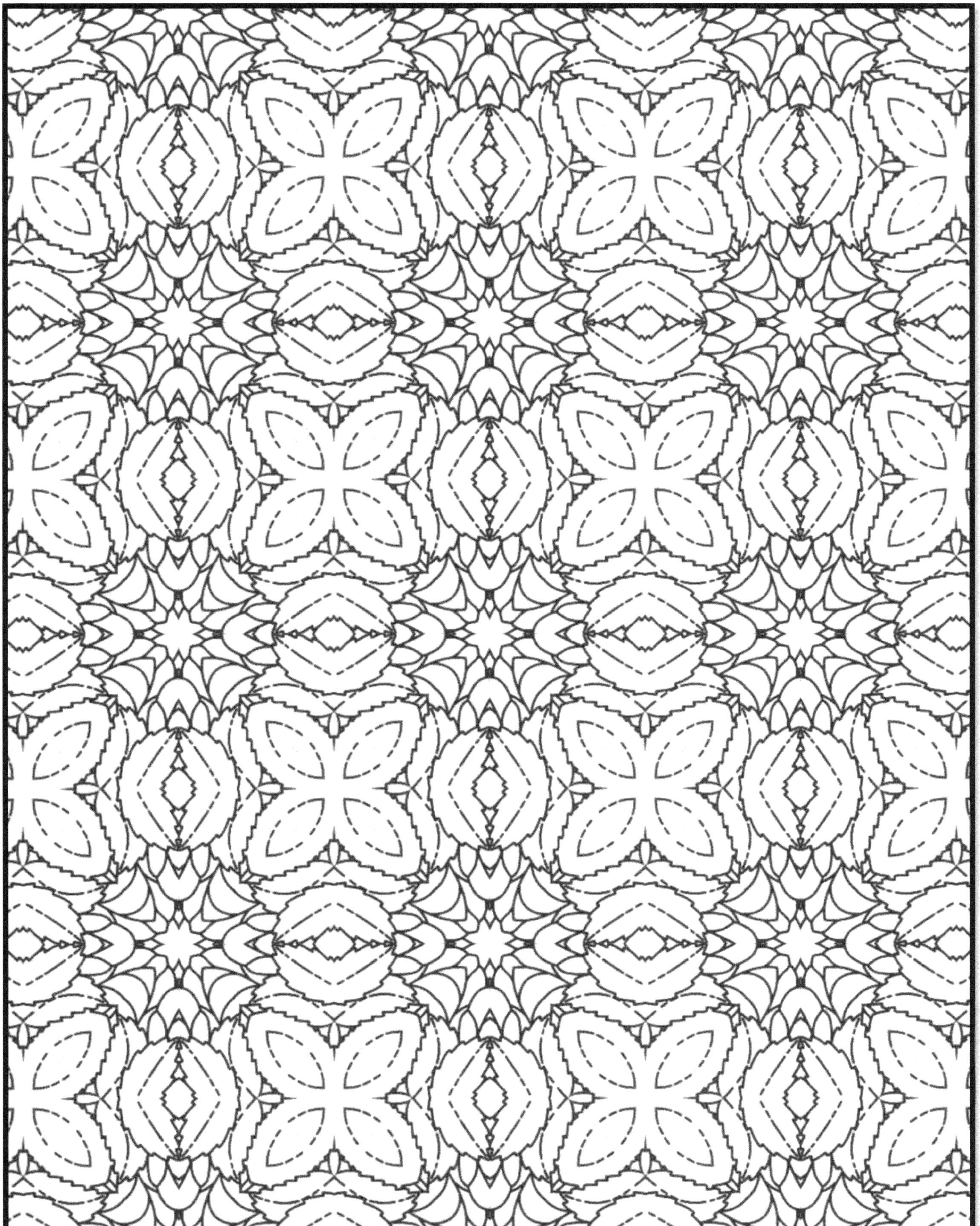

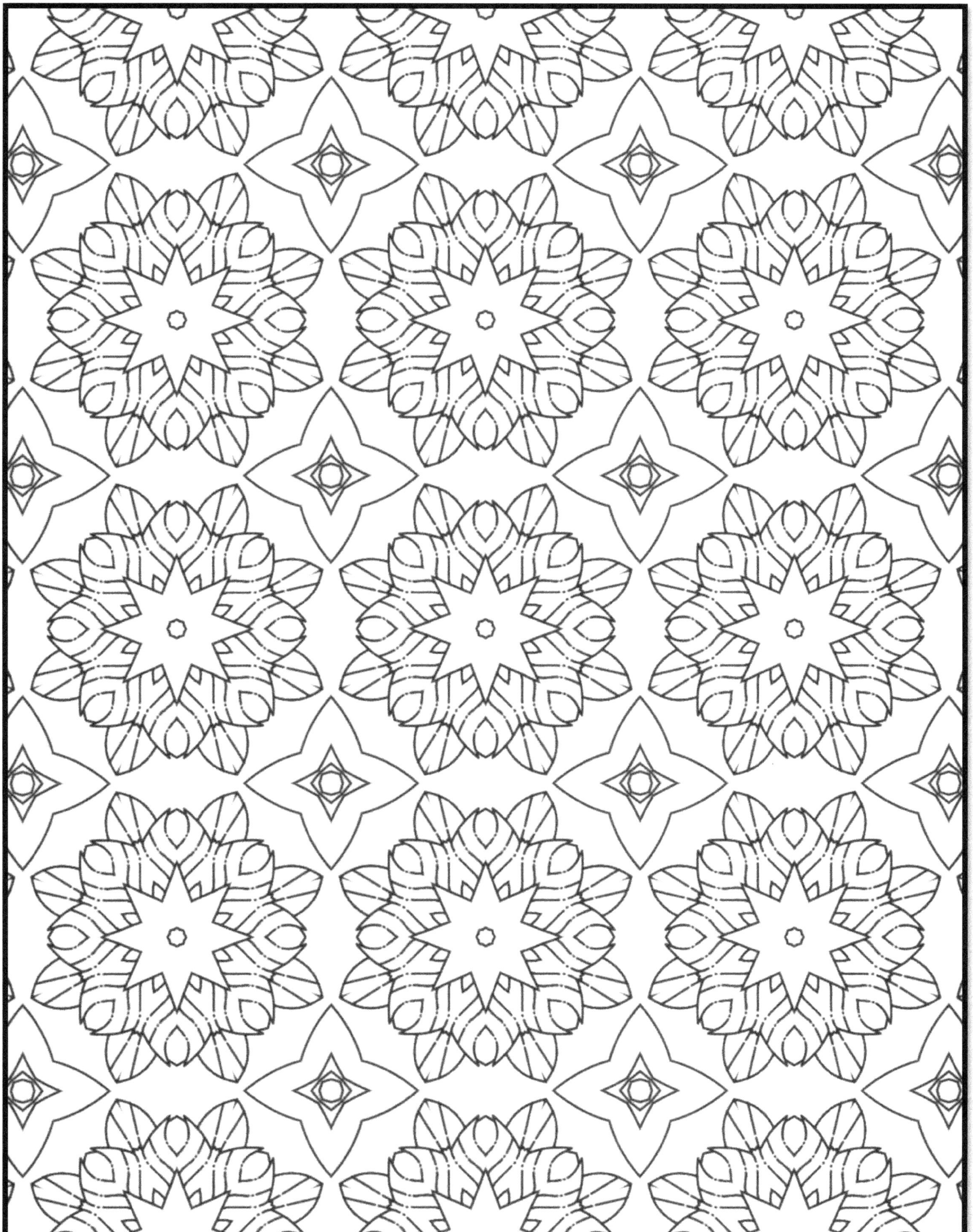

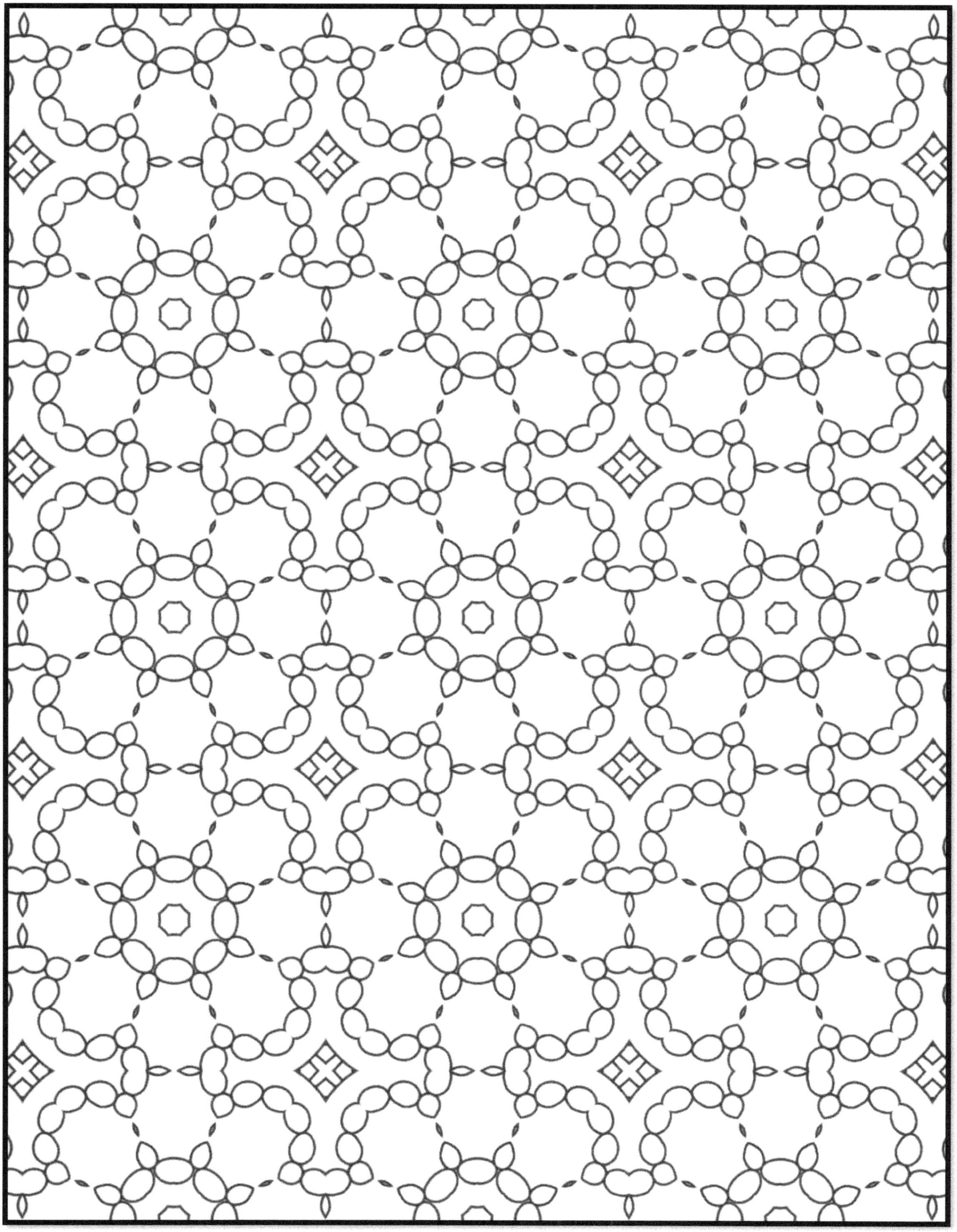

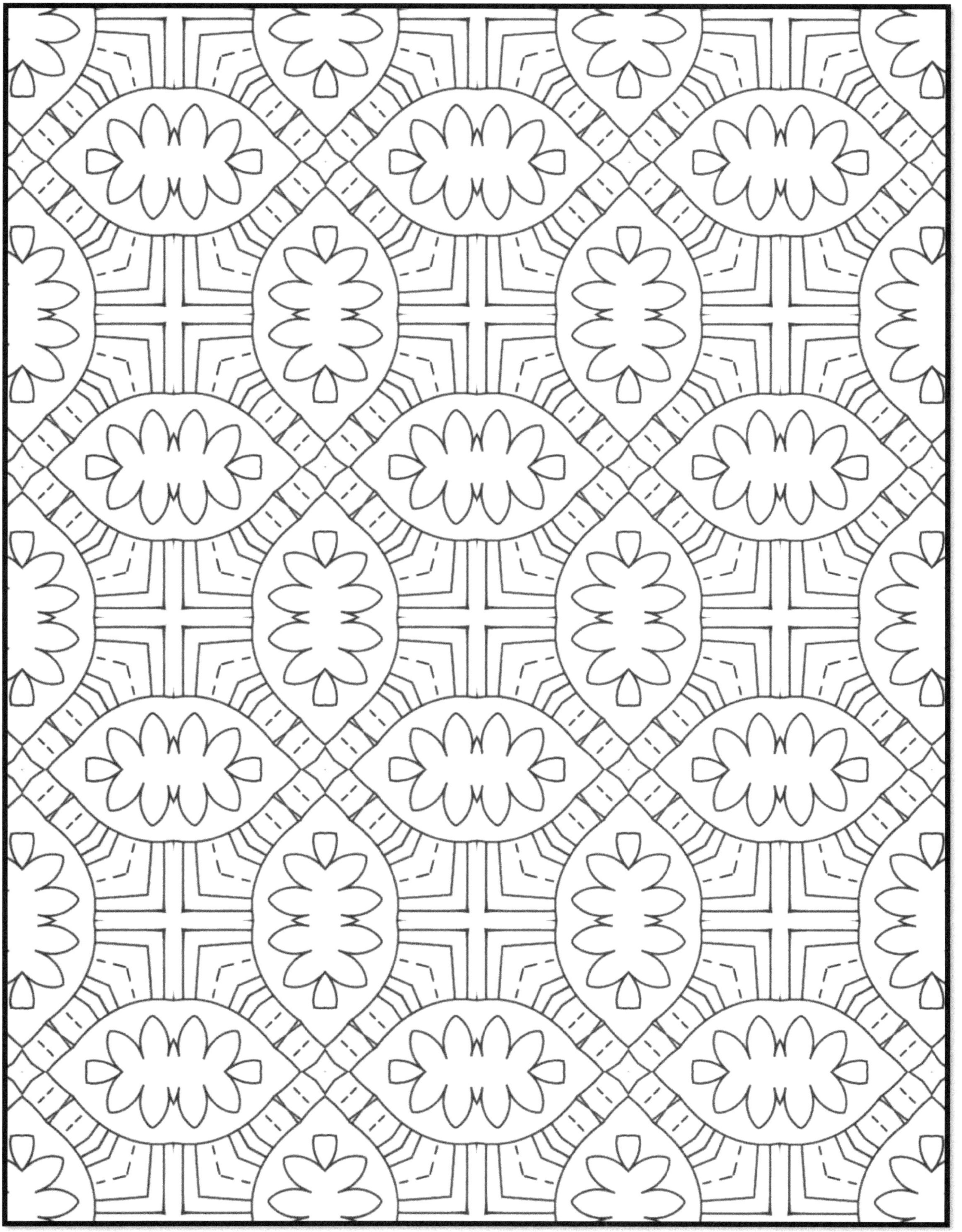

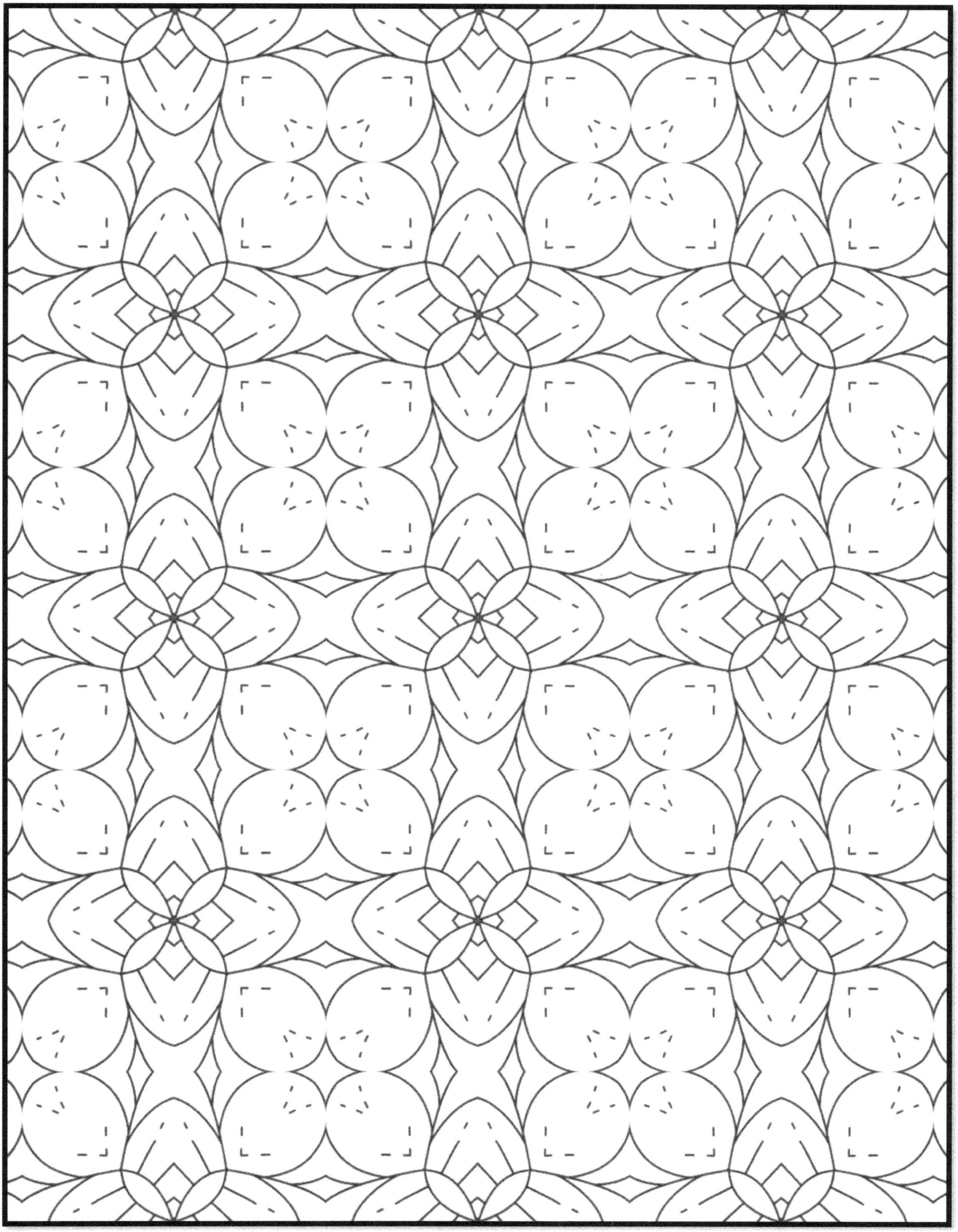

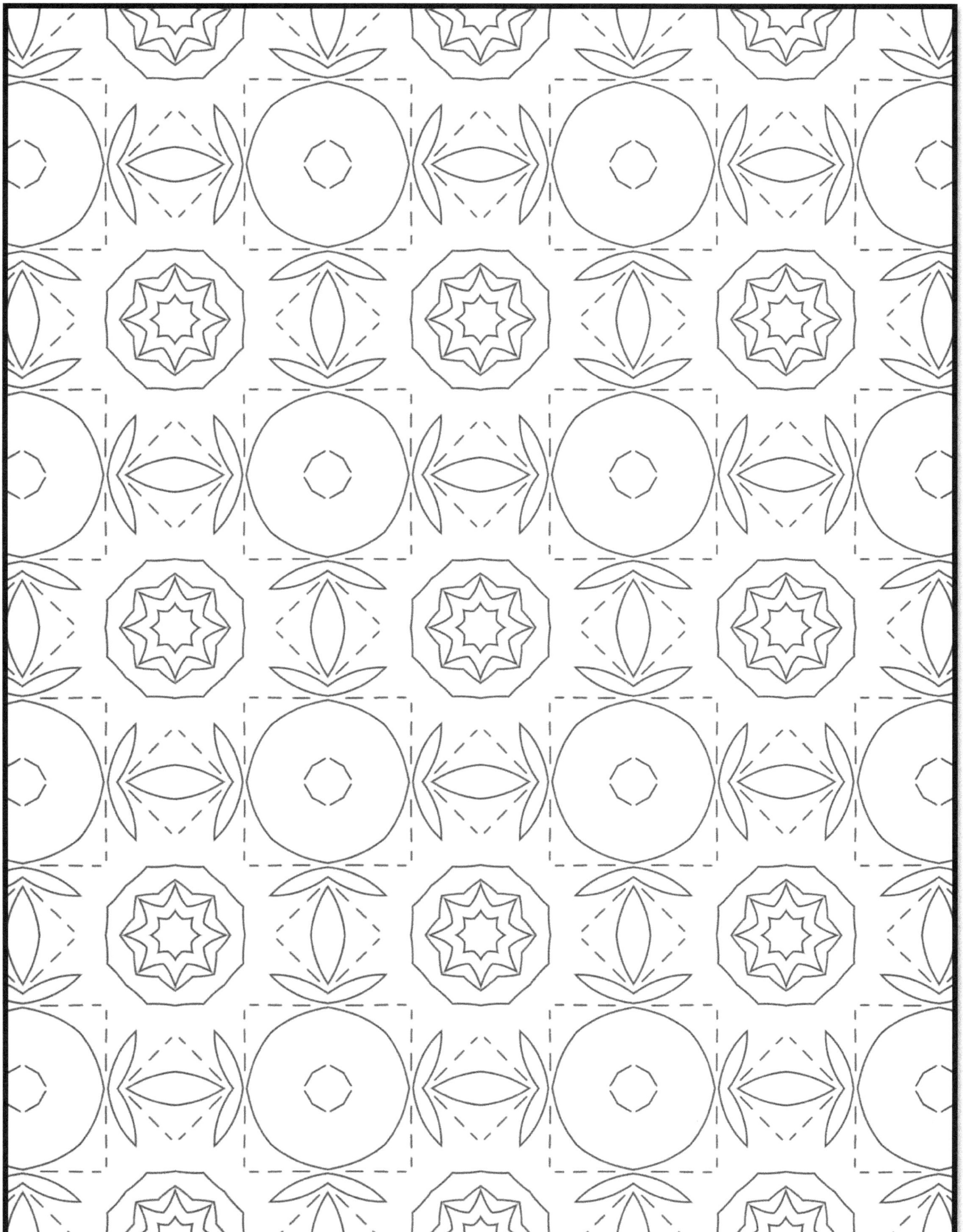

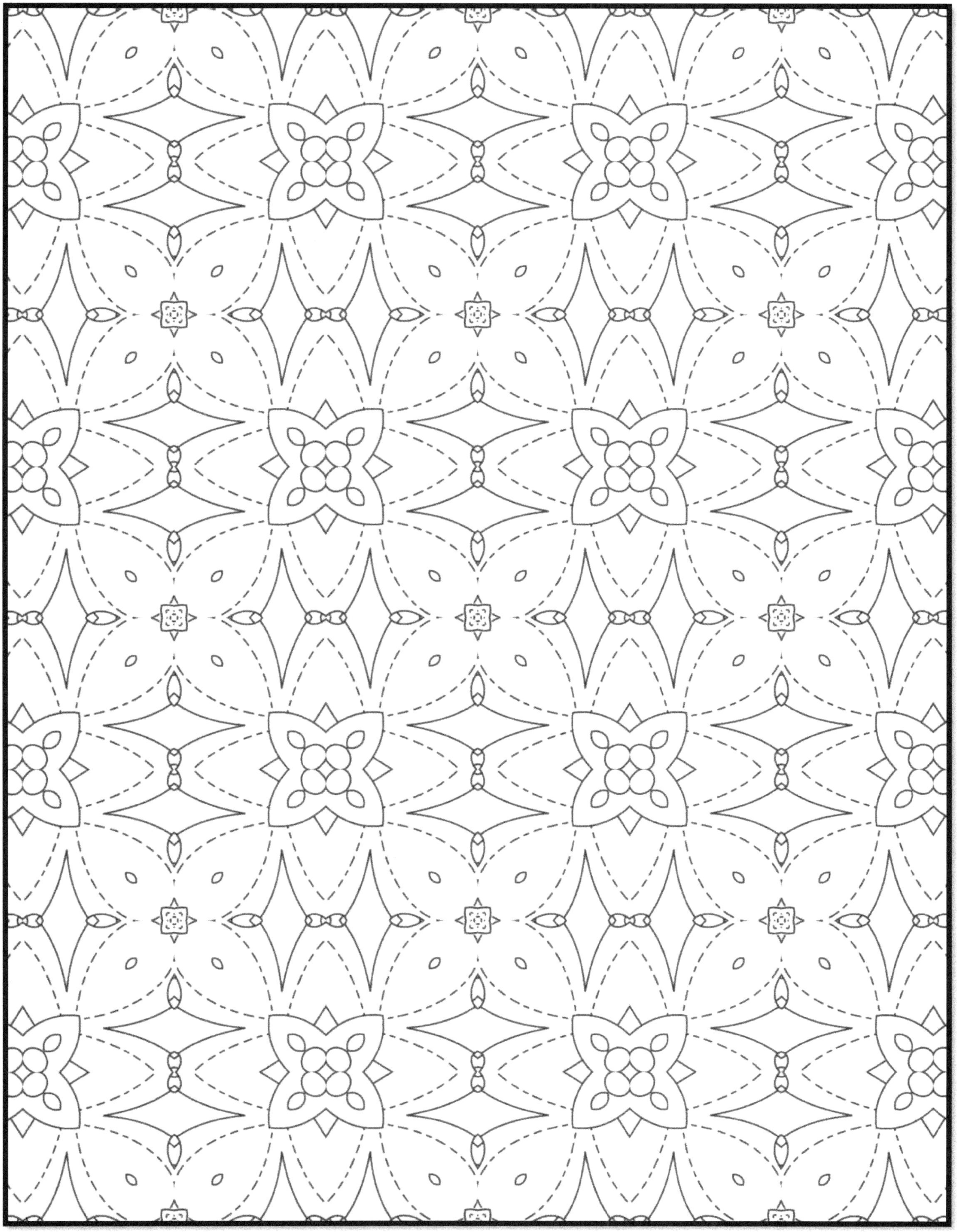

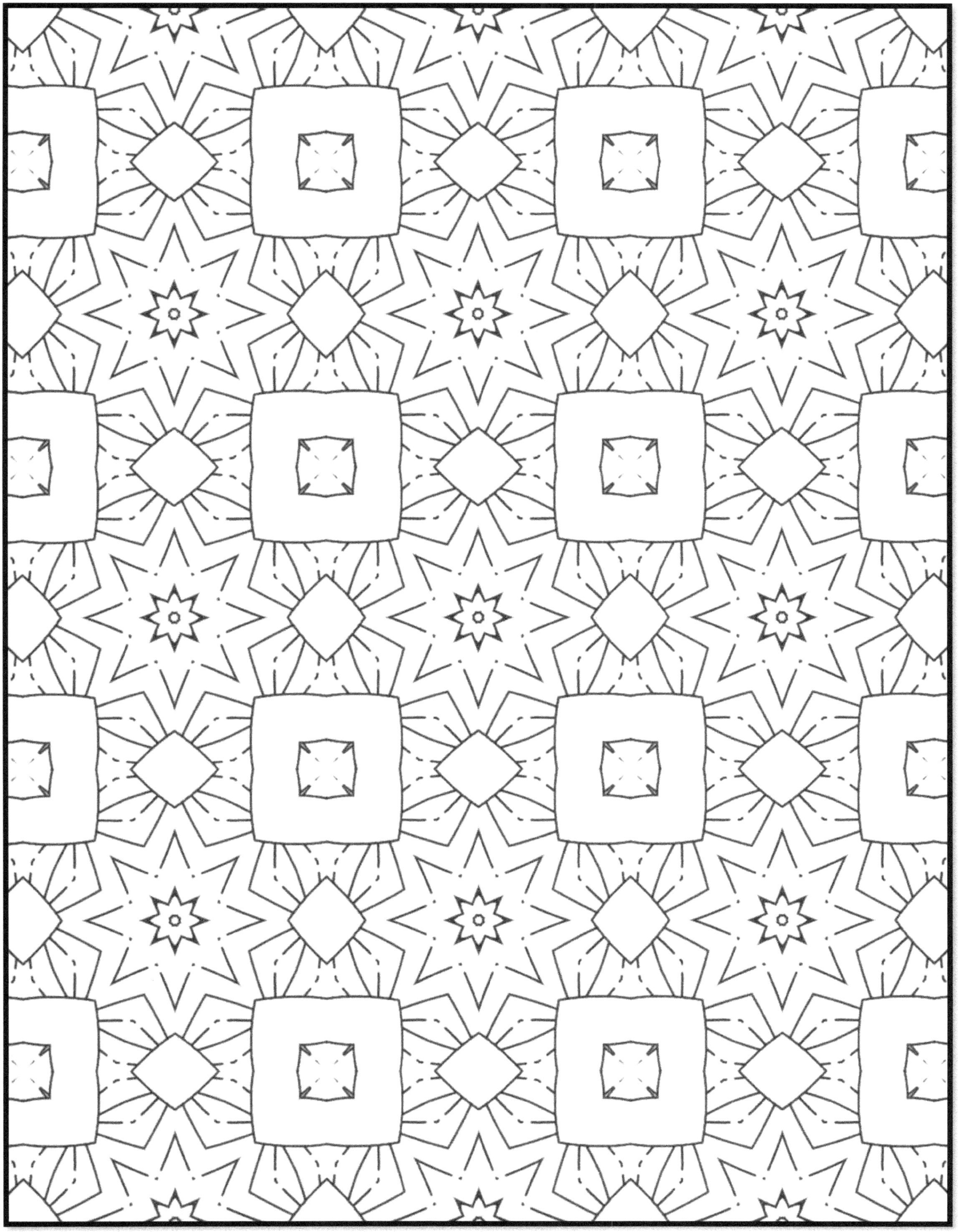

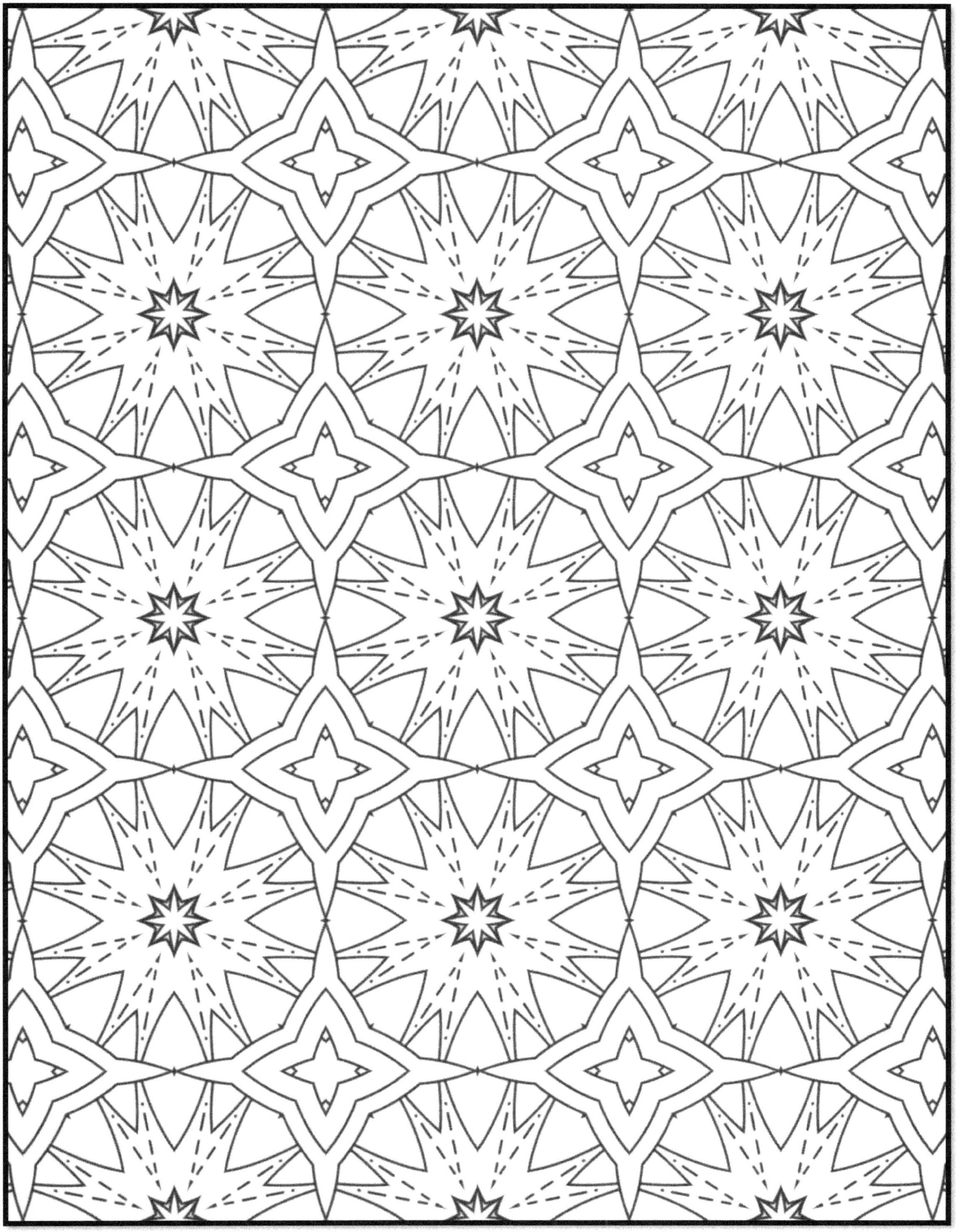

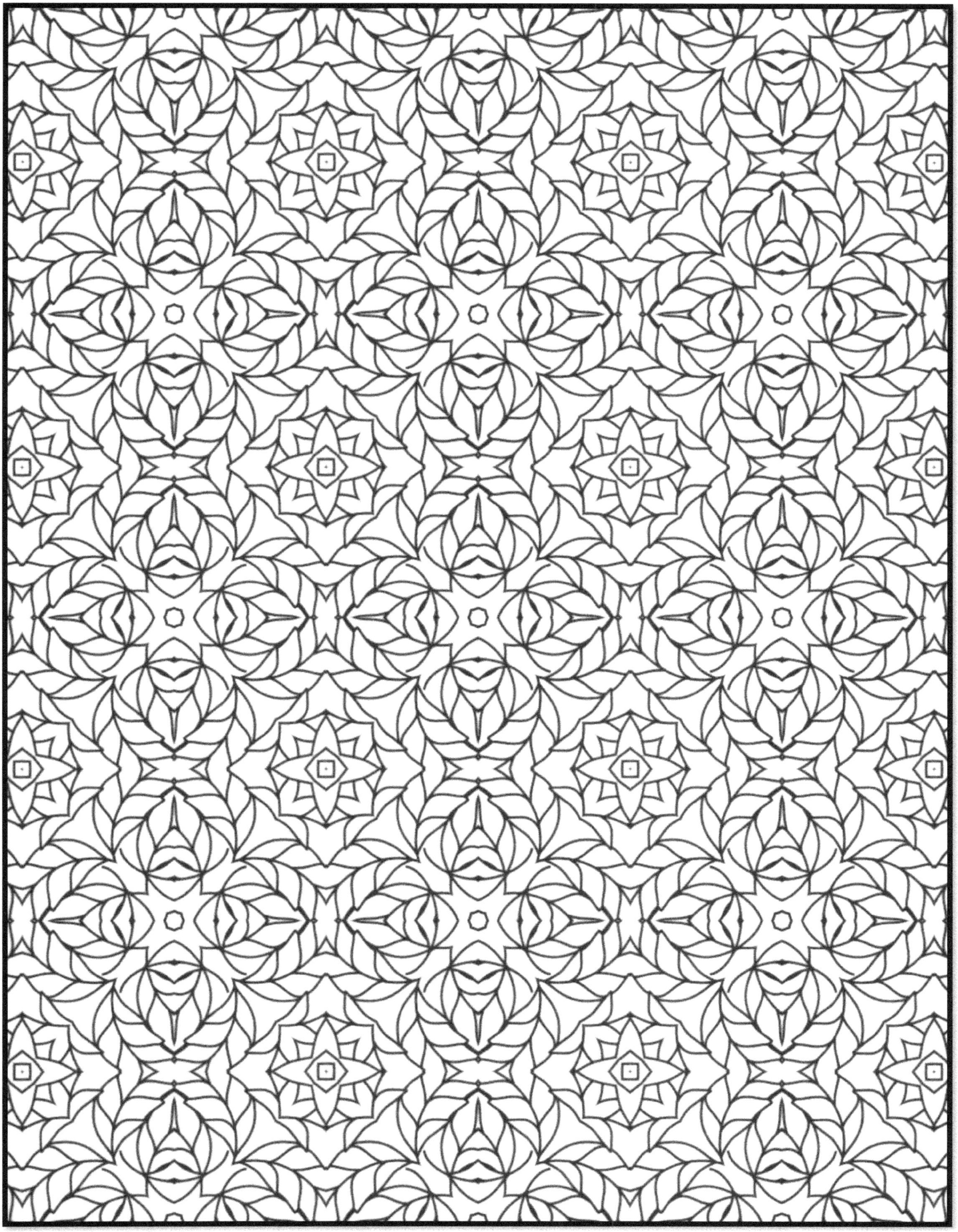

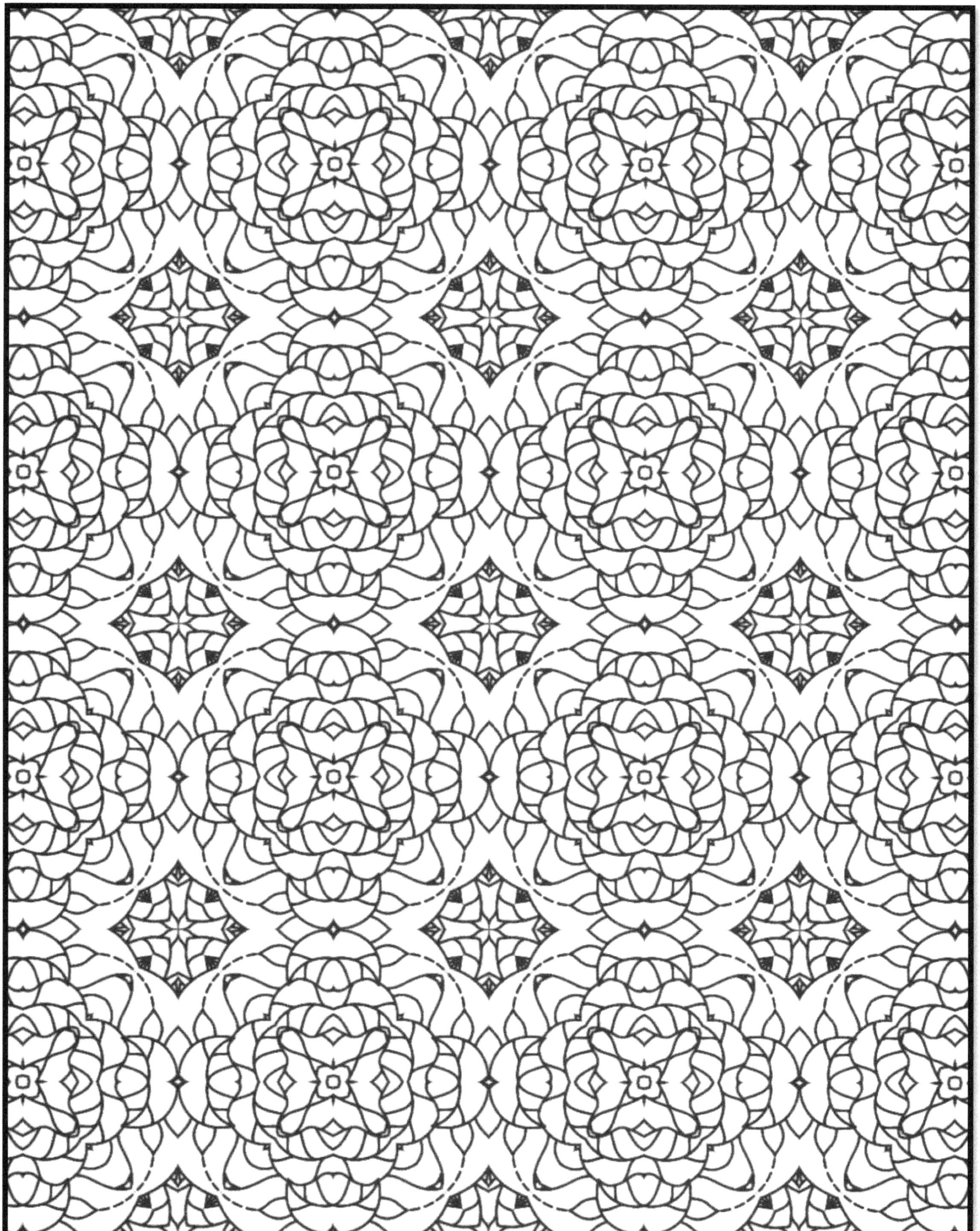

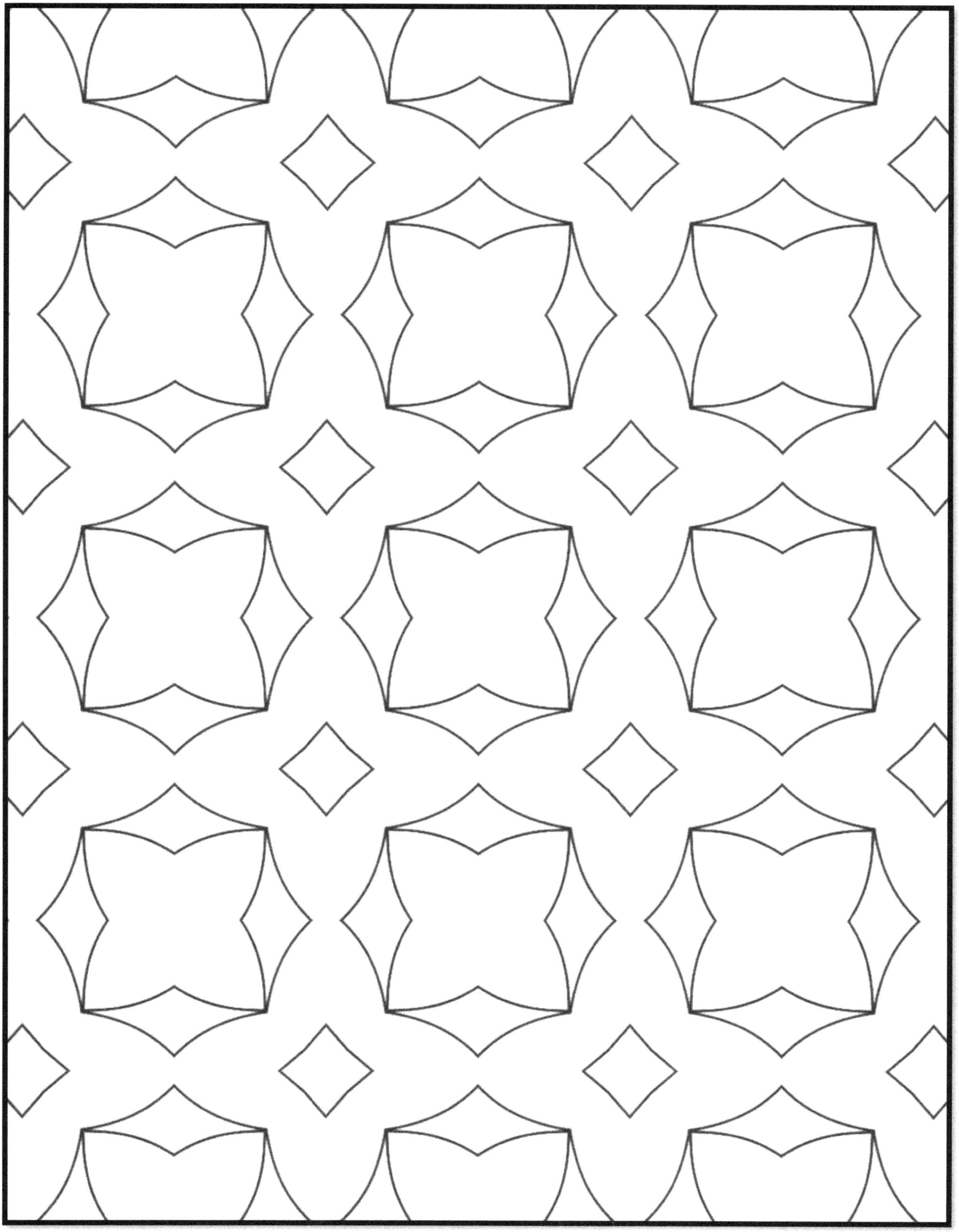

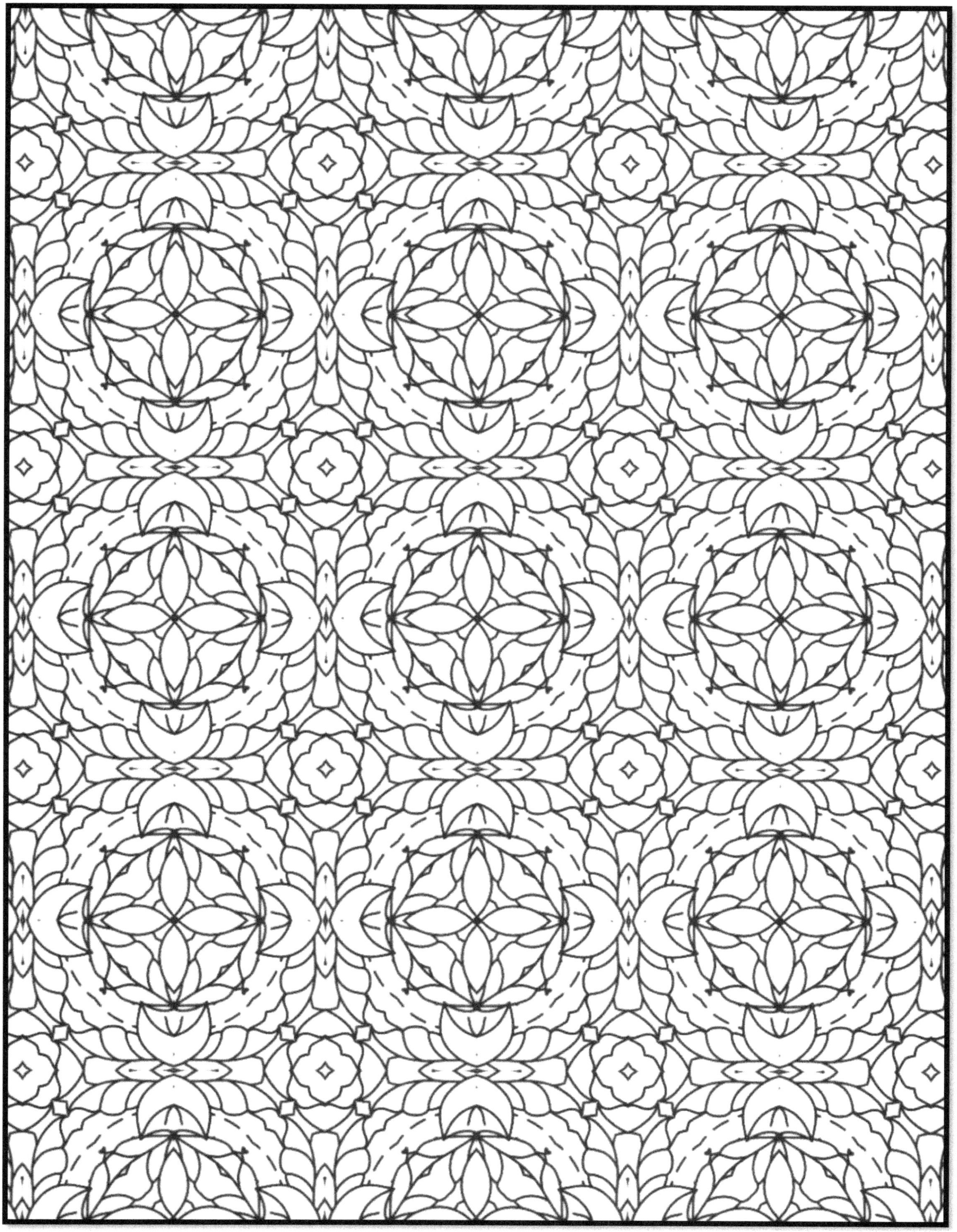

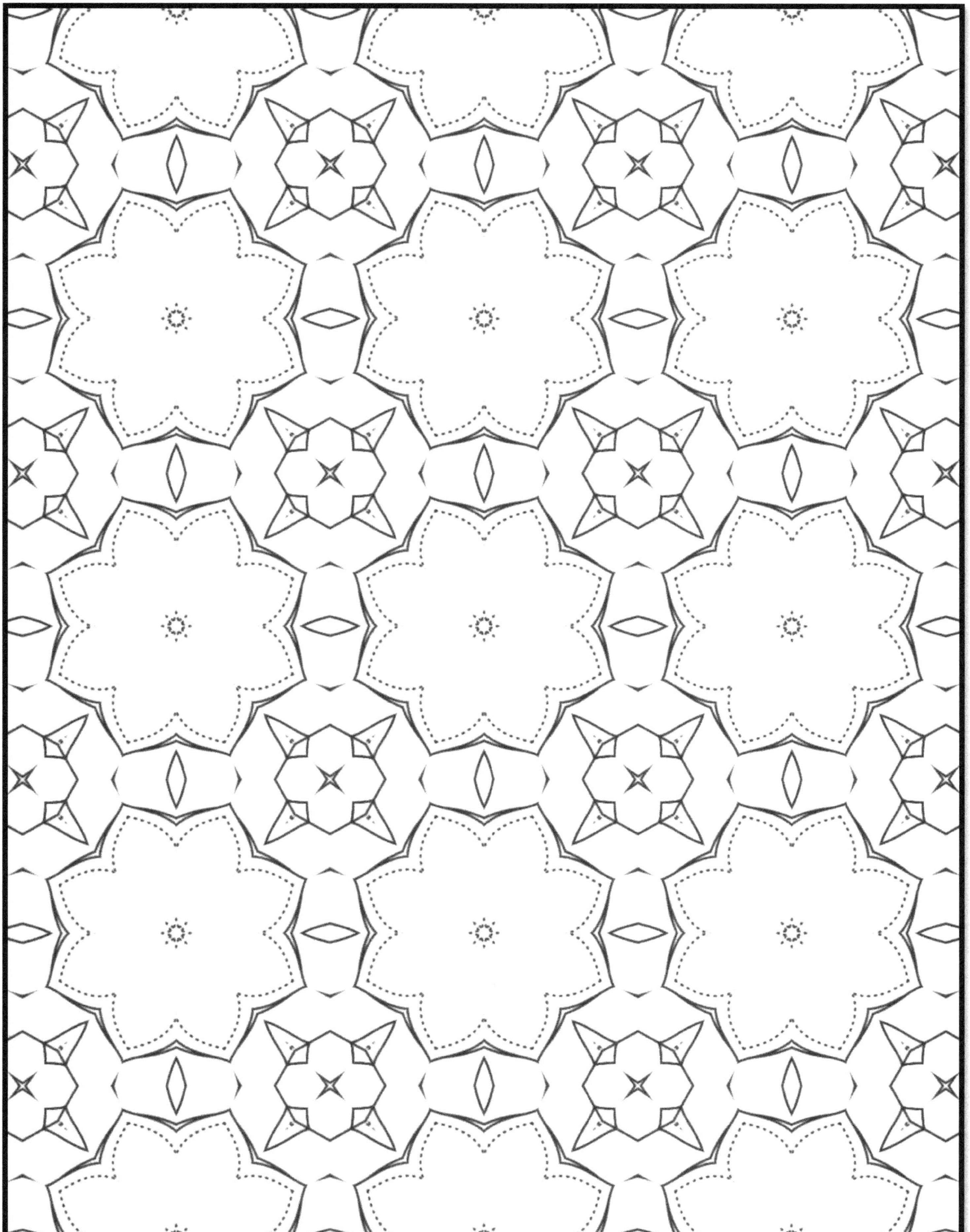

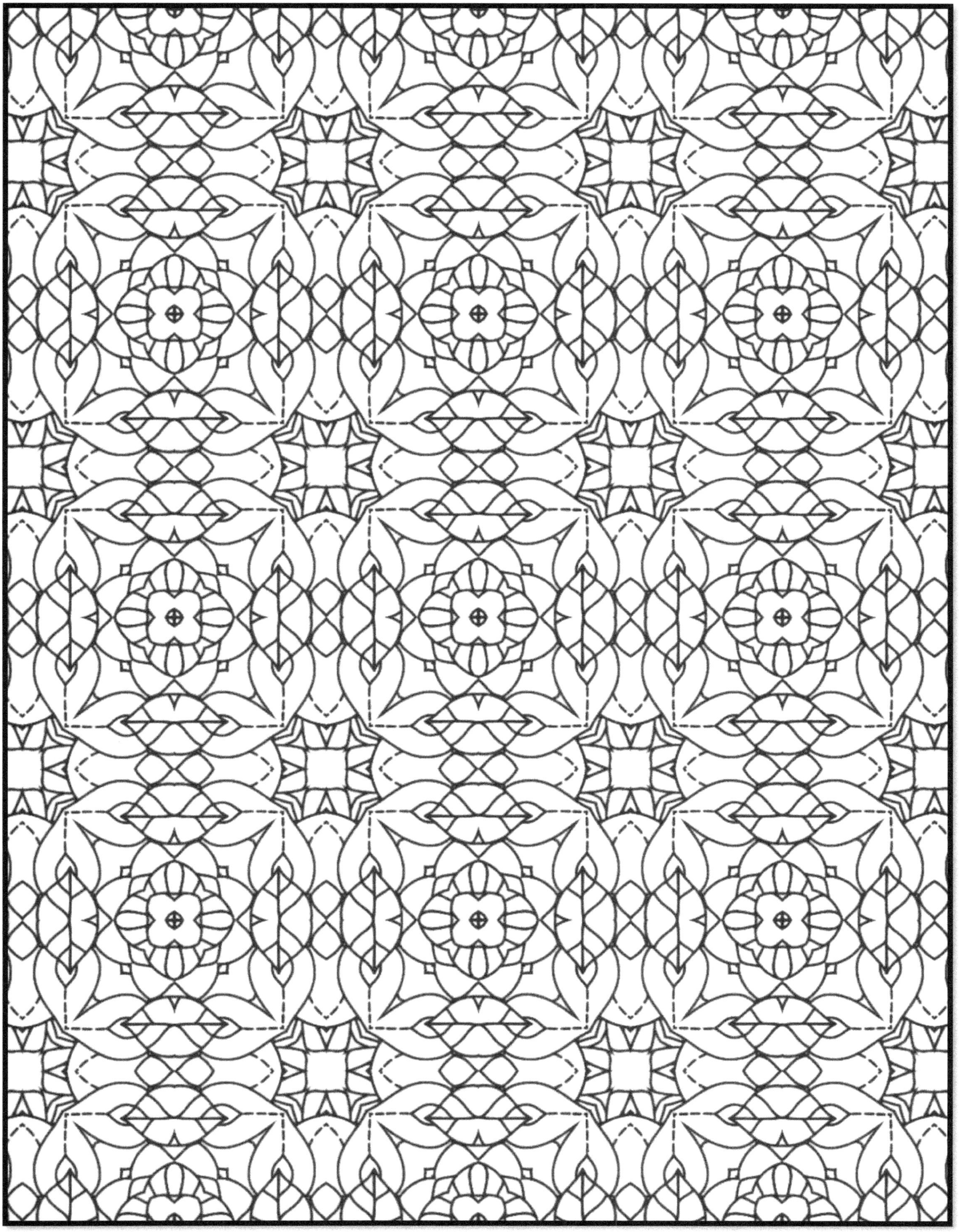

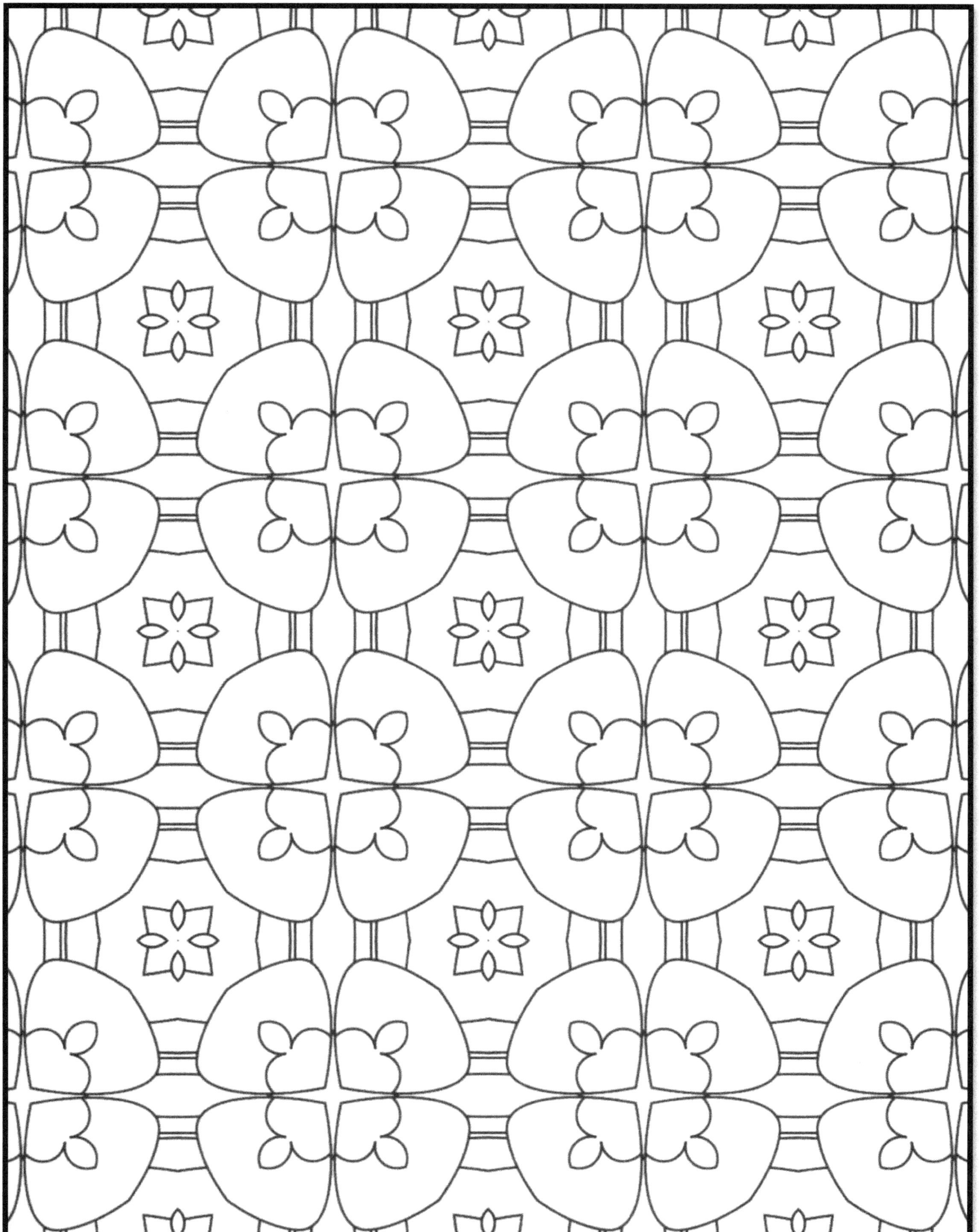

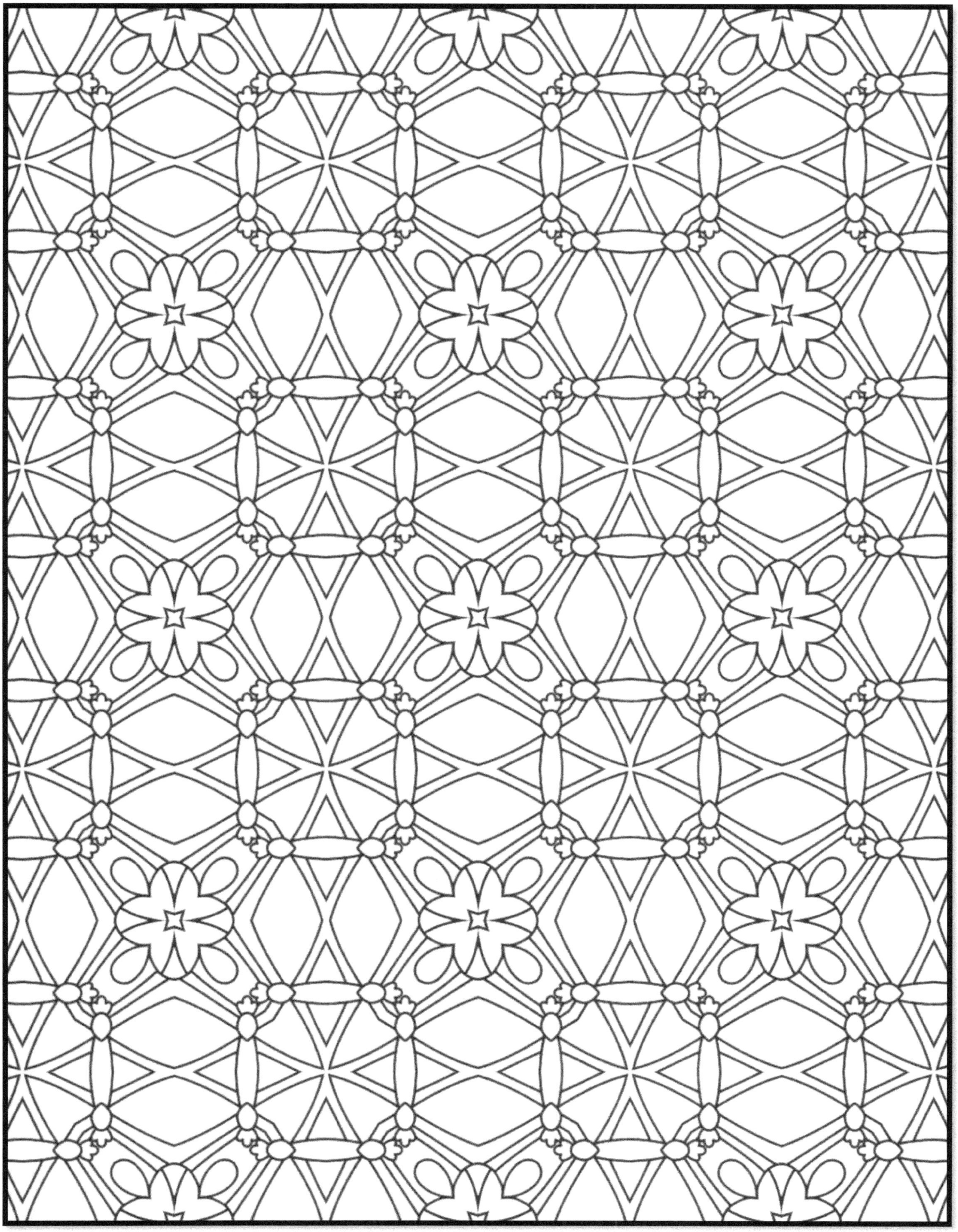

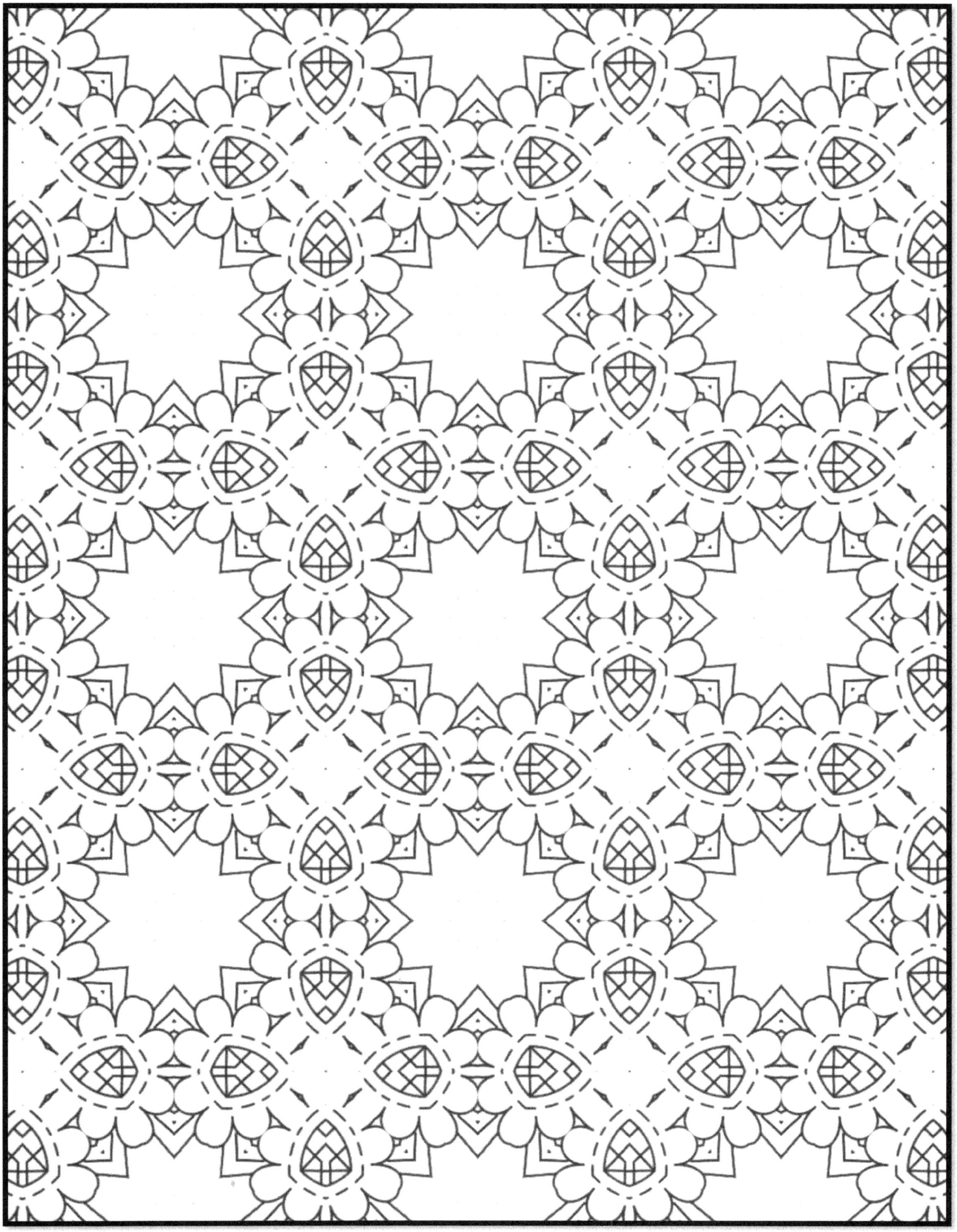

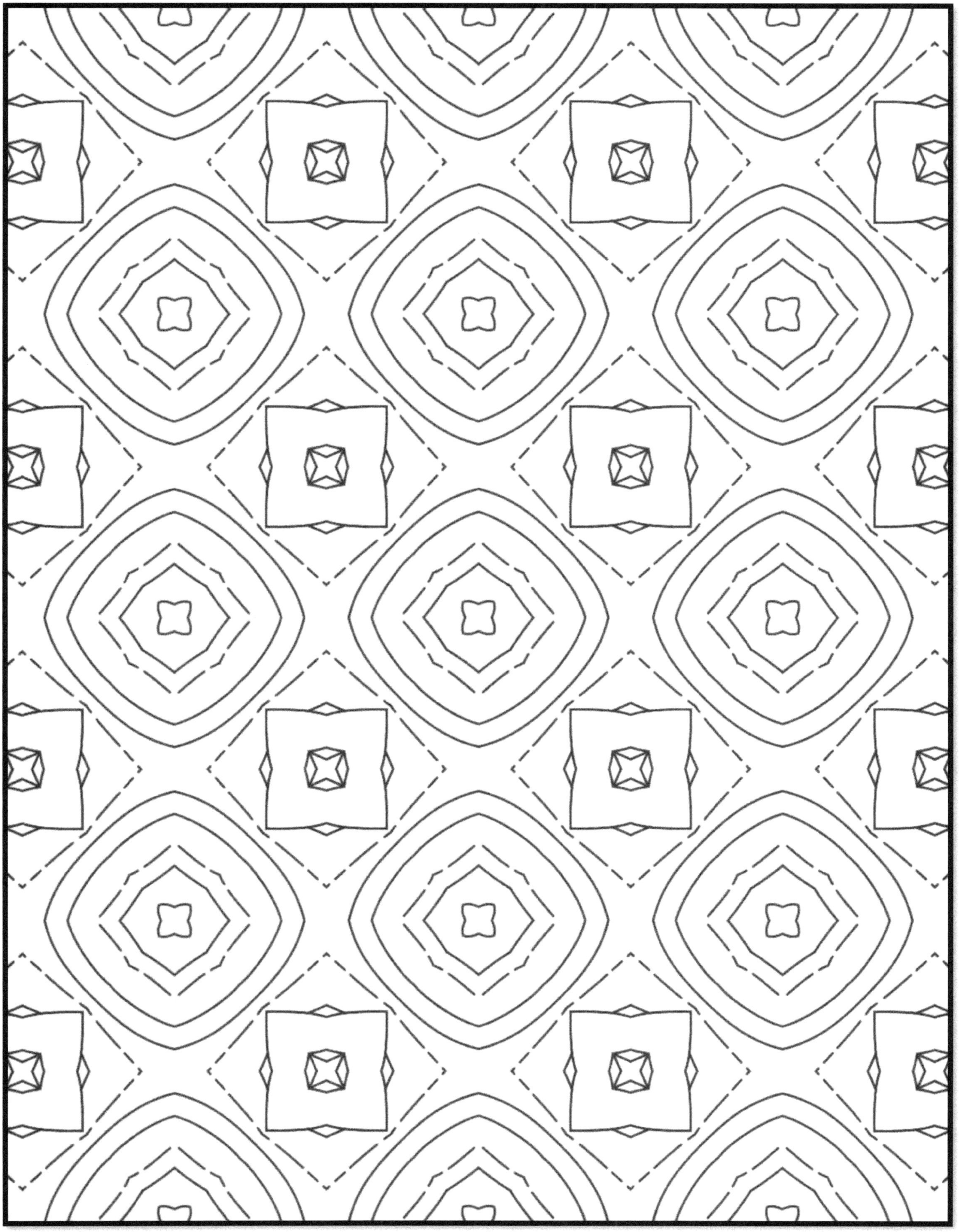

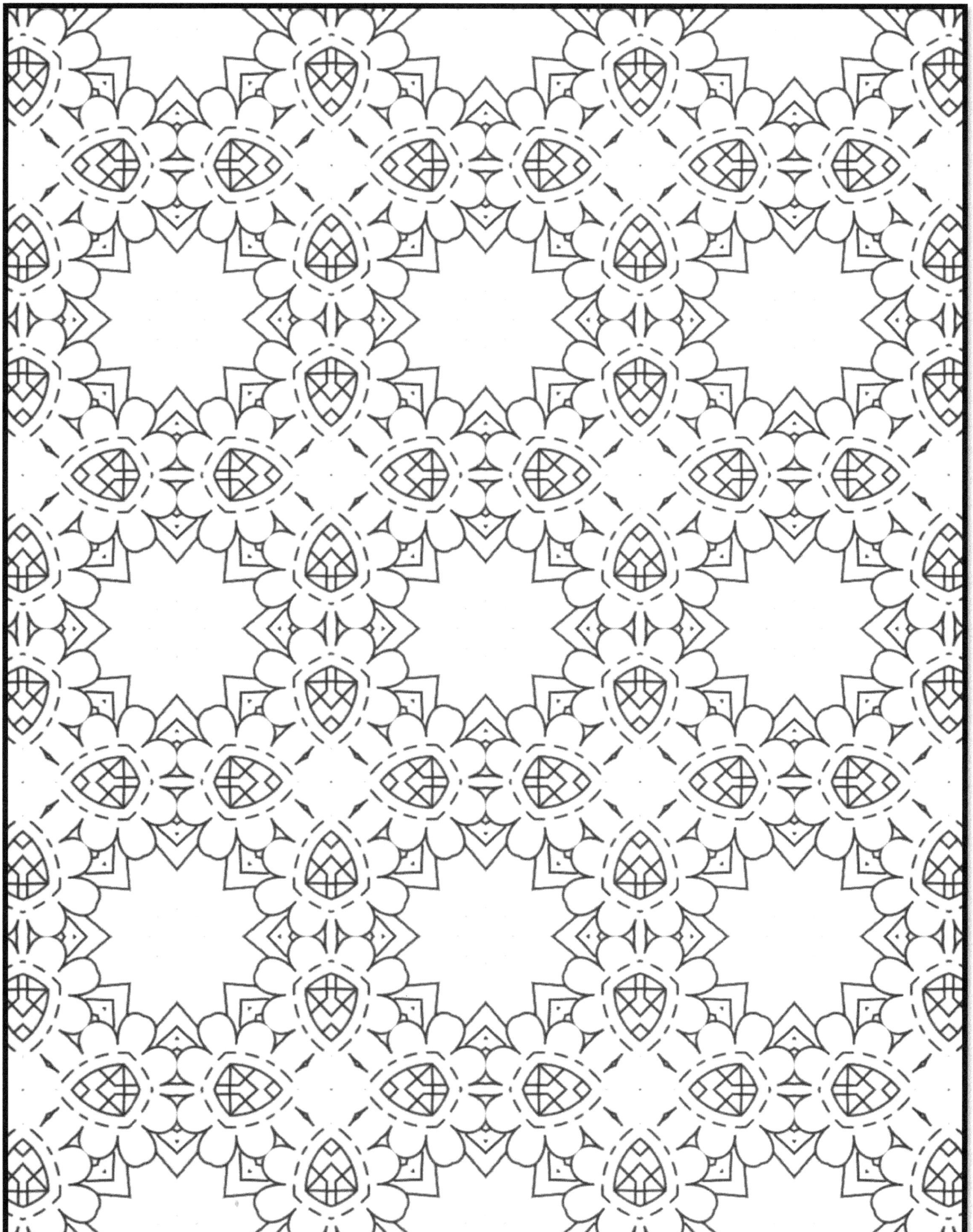

CPSIA information can be obtained
at www.ICGtesting.com
Printed in the USA
LVHW061108110622
721053LV00027B/795

9 798596 652871